@RosenTeenTalk

# DIABETES

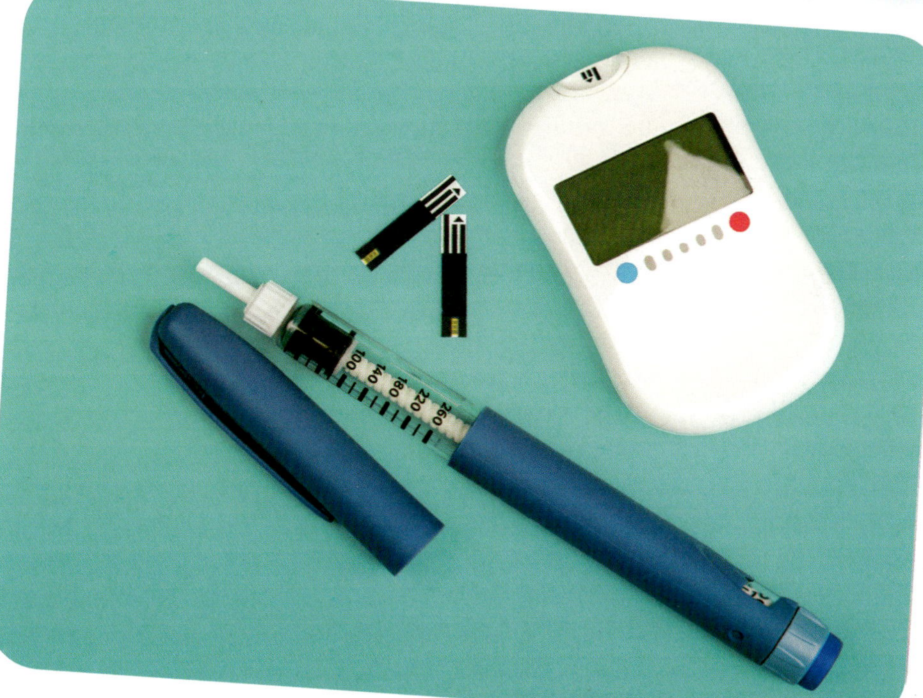

Jodyanne Benson

NEW YORK

Published in 2021 by The Rosen Publishing Group, Inc.
29 East 21st Street, New York, NY 10010



First Edition



Editor: Elizabeth Krajnik
Designer: Michael Flynn
Interior Layout: Rachel Rising

Photo Credits: Cover, p. 1 Fuss Sergey/Shutterstock.com; cover Cosmic_Design/Shutterstock.com; cover, pp. 3, 5, 10, 45, New Africa/Shutterstock.com; cover, pp. 1, 6, 8, 10, 12, 16, 18, 20, 24, 26, 28, 30, 34, 36, 38, 40, 42 Vitya_M/Shutterstock.com; pp. 3, 15 Daisy Daisy/Shutterstock.com; pp. 3, 23 Quality Stock Arts/Shutterstock .com; pp. 3, 33 Ron Levine/DigitalVision/Getty Images; p. 6 Muza_Art/Shutterstock.com; p. 7 Rawpixel.com/ Shutterstock.com; p. 8 Africa Studio/Shutterstock.com; p. 9 Double Brain/Shutterstock.com; p. 11 Eviart/ Shutterstock.com; p. 12 OMMB/Shutterstock.com; p. 13 Yevgen Romanenko/Moment/Getty Images; p. 16 Motortion Films/Shutterstock.com; p. 17 Happy Together/Shutterstock.com; p. 18 bitt24/Shutterstock.com; p. 19 stockcreations/Shutterstock.com; p. 21 sturti/E+/Getty Images; p. 24 HRAUN/E+/Getty Images; p. 25 lithian/Shutterstock.com; p. 26 Science Photo Library/Getty Images; p. 28 Pressmaster/Shutterstock.com; p. 29 aldomurillo/E+/Getty Images; p. 31 Samuel Borges Photography/Shuttterstock.com; p. 34 Dmitry Lobanov/ Shutterstock.com; p. 35 Maya Kruchankova/Shutterstock.com; p. 36 Fuse/Corbis/Getty Images; p. 37 Eugene Powers/Shutterstock.com; p. 38 Obradovic/E+/Getty Images; p. 41 Comstock Images/Stockbyte/Getty Images; p. 42 Jon Feingersh Photography Inc/DigitalVision/Getty Images.

Some of the images in this book illustrate individuals who are models. The depictions do not imply actual situations or events.

Library of Congress Cataloging-in-Publication Data

Names: Benson, Jodyanne, author.
Title: Diabetes / Jodyanne Benson.
Description: New York : Rosen Publishing, [2021] | Series: @rosenteentalk | Includes index.
Identifiers: LCCN 2019059402 | ISBN 9781499468120 (paperback) | ISBN 9781499468137 (library binding)
Subjects: LCSH: Diabetes in adolescence—Juvenile literature.
Classification: LCC RJ420.D5 B44 2021 | DDC 618.92/4624—dc23
LC record available at https://lccn.loc.gov/2019059402

Manufactured in the United States of America

CPSIA Compliance Information: Batch #BSR20. For further information contact Rosen Publishing, New York, New York at 1-800-237-9932.

# CONTENTS

## Chapter 1

# Diabetes Changed My Life

When I was 12 years old, my doctor **diagnosed** me with type 1 diabetes. I didn't know what diabetes was or how it would change my life. I didn't know anyone with diabetes. I felt scared and alone.

My friends didn't seem to understand diabetes or what I was going through. During lunch, they would ask if I could eat sugar. They thought I got diabetes from eating too much sugar when I was younger.

I became very upset and **embarrassed** when I'd have to check my blood sugar at school. One day, my blood sugar got so low that I needed to go to the hospital. After that, I became very worried about everything I ate.

When I was younger, I'd test my blood sugar out in the hallway instead of in the classroom or at the lunch table. I felt like I had to hide my health condition from my friends.

# WHAT IS DIABETES?

Diabetes is a chronic, or long-lasting, condition. It affects how the body uses glucose. Glucose is a type of sugar found in plants and fruits. Our bodies use glucose for **energy**. When we eat, our blood sugar goes up. This tells the **pancreas** to make **insulin**.

The two main types of diabetes are type 1 and type 2. Type 1 diabetes is when the pancreas doesn't make enough insulin. Type 2 diabetes is when the body doesn't use insulin as well as it should.

November 14 is World Diabetes Day. The blue circle is the **symbol** used around the world for diabetes.

WORLD DIABETES DAY

# What Causes Diabetes?

Scientists think **genes** and harmful things in the **environment**, such as **viruses**, cause type 1 diabetes.

Type 2 diabetes is caused by lifestyle issues, such as unhealthy eating and not exercising. Genes and family history can also cause type 2 diabetes.

## FACTS AND FIGURES

- In 2015, about 23 million adults in the United States had diagnosed diabetes.
- Type 2 diabetes is much more common than type 1 diabetes.
- Diabetes is most **prevalent** in Mississippi, West Virginia, Louisiana, Texas, South Carolina, Alabama, and Georgia.
- Diabetes is least prevalent in Vermont, Minnesota, Montana, and Colorado.

# HOW IS DIABETES DIAGNOSED?

Doctors can find out if someone has diabetes by testing how much glucose is in their blood. High amounts of glucose usually means the person has diabetes. Doctors can run more tests to find out which type of diabetes the person has.

Sometimes doctors run another blood test called the glycated hemoglobin (hemoglobin A1c or HbA1c) test. It measures the person's average blood sugar level over the course of about two to three months before the test. It can also tell doctors how well a person is managing their diabetes.

A pediatric endocrinologist is a doctor who specializes in diagnosing and treating children who have diabetes and other endocrine conditions.

# What Is the Endocrine System?

The pancreas is part of the endocrine system. The endocrine system is the group of **glands** that make **hormones**. Hormones help organs and systems of the body talk to each other.

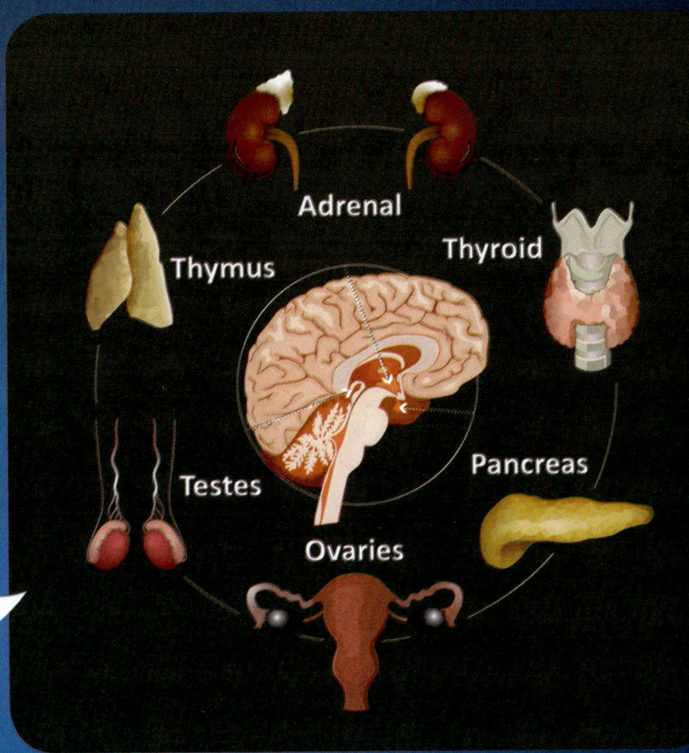


## DID YOU KNOW?

- Type 1 diabetes can **develop** at any time but is usually diagnosed in children, teens, and young adults. This is why it used to be called juvenile diabetes.
- Type 2 diabetes is more commonly diagnosed in adults over 45 years old. However, more children, teens, and young adults are developing type 2 diabetes.

# WHAT IS TYPE 1 DIABETES?

When someone has type 1 diabetes, their pancreas can't make or makes very little insulin. Insulin is the hormone that allows blood sugar to enter the cells of the body. Without insulin, blood sugar can't get into cells. Our cells need blood sugar for energy.

As a result, blood sugar builds up in the bloodstream. This causes high blood sugar, which makes people sick. People with type 1 diabetes need to take insulin shots or wear an insulin pump every day.

People with diabetes need different supplies to control their blood sugar levels.

# Did You Know?

In the United States, type 1 diabetes is more common in white people than in African Americans and Hispanic/Latino Americans.

People are more likely to develop type 1 diabetes if they have a parent, brother, or sister with diabetes.

## SYMPTOMS OF TYPE 1 DIABETES

- Peeing a lot, especially at night, because the body needs to get rid of the extra blood sugar
- Nausea (feeling like you're going to vomit)
- Extreme thirst
- Losing weight without trying
- Feeling tired
- Extreme hunger
- Stomach pains
- Vomiting

# HOW IS TYPE 1 DIABETES TREATED?

It's very important that people with type 1 diabetes get treatment. It can help make symptoms better and prevent other health problems, including death. Treatment can also help people stay **physically** and **emotionally** healthy.

Some people wear an insulin pump instead of giving themselves shots. The pump sends insulin into the body throughout the day and when the person eats.

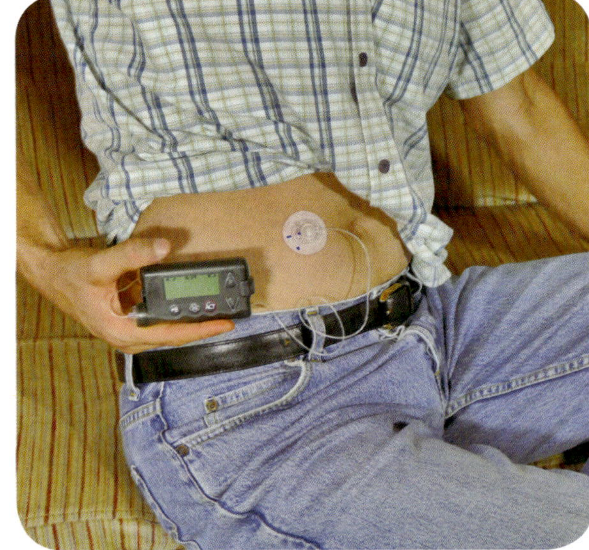

Most people with type 1 diabetes need to check their blood sugar and take insulin shots every day. They can also control their blood sugar levels by eating healthy foods, exercising, getting enough sleep, and managing **stress**.

## Hypoglycemia vs. Hyperglycemia

Hypoglycemia is when your blood sugar is low. Hyperglycemia is when your blood sugar is high.

## INSULIN TYPES

Insulin types are different based on how long they take to start working and how long they last. Someone may use more than one type of insulin.

- Rapid-acting insulin starts working within 15 minutes.
- Short-acting insulin starts working within 30 minutes.
- Intermediate-acting insulin starts working within about 1 to 3 hours and lasts 12 to 24 hours.
- Long and ultra-long-acting insulin works for 14 to 40 hours.

Chapter 2

# Struggling to Manage

I was diagnosed with type 1 diabetes when I was 10 years old. My parents helped me a lot with managing my diabetes when I was younger and through middle school. They kept track of my blood glucose levels and adjusted how much insulin I needed. The school nurse also helped a lot.

When I started high school, I struggled to manage my diabetes on my own. So, a year ago, I started using an insulin pump. It's made my life easier in a lot of ways.

Lately I've been forgetting to check my blood sugar. This makes my parents upset. With school and activities, I feel too busy to keep up with managing my diabetes. I wish I didn't have diabetes.

My parents reminded me that if I remember to test my blood sugar and stay on top of my insulin shots, I'll have more energy to play sports and be able to think more clearly.

# WHAT IS TYPE 2 DIABETES?

When someone has type 2 diabetes, their pancreas still makes insulin. But the cells in their body can't process and use it normally. This is called insulin resistance. The pancreas makes more insulin because it knows there's too much glucose in the blood.

One-third of young people in America are overweight. Being overweight is linked to type 2 diabetes. The first step in preventing type 2 diabetes is maintaining a healthy weight. Regular exercise is one way to do that.

As a result, the pancreas works even harder to make more insulin. Eventually, the pancreas may get tired of working so hard. This means it won't be able to make enough insulin to control the person's blood sugar.

## Did You Know?

More than 75 percent of kids with type 2 diabetes have a family member who also has it.

**Data** from 2014 estimates that more than 5,000 new cases of type 2 diabetes are diagnosed in people younger than 20 years old each year.

## SIGNS OF TYPE 2 DIABETES

- Peeing a lot to get rid of the extra glucose in the body
- Drinking a lot because the person is peeing so much
- Feeling tired because the body doesn't turn glucose into energy

# HOW IS TYPE 2 DIABETES TREATED?

Type 2 diabetes is treated by eating healthy foods and exercising. People with type 2 diabetes have to check their blood sugar. Some people with type 2 diabetes need insulin and other medicines to manage their blood sugar.

People with diabetes need to count **carbohydrates**. Carbohydrates break down into glucose. To learn how to count carbohydrates, people can work with a **dietitian**.

Young people with type 2 diabetes need to see a doctor regularly. The doctor will tell them how often they need to check their blood sugar. If they need insulin, they'll need to check their blood sugar more often.

## Let's Get Active!

Children over six years old should be active for at least an hour each day. Most of this hour should be aerobic exercise. This is exercise that gets your heart and lungs working hard. You can go for a nature hike, a bike ride, or a swim.

## HEALTHY BITES!

Eating healthy foods helps keep blood sugar within target range:

- Fruits, vegetables, whole grains, and legumes (such as beans and peas) are healthy carbohydrates and fiber-rich foods.
- Brussels sprouts, chia seeds, walnuts, and flaxseeds are foods rich in omega-3 fatty acids, which can help prevent heart disease.
- Avocados, nuts, and olive oil are good fats and can help lower **cholesterol** levels.

# LIFE CHANGES AFFECT HEALTH

People experience many physical, emotional, and social changes in their teenage years. They want to feel independent and like they fit in. It can be hard for young people to manage diabetes when they have activities, school, and even jobs.

Treating diabetes is a big responsibility. Checking your blood sugar may feel like it's getting in the way. But it's always important to stay on top of your blood sugar. This will keep you healthy for many years to come.

It's important to talk to trusted adults and doctors about your diabetes. They can help you find ways to manage your diabetes that work for you.

Chapter 3

# Making a Change

I've always struggled with my weight and eating healthy. When I was 14 years old, my doctor diagnosed me with type 2 diabetes. I never thought that I'd be diagnosed with such a serious disease.

My doctor was really honest with me. He told me about the health problems I could have later in life if I didn't get my diabetes under control. Then and there, I decided to make a change.

My parents and I started eating healthier meals and spending more time exercising. We don't watch much TV anymore. My dad and I play catch in the afternoons when we get home. I do yoga in my room before school each day to get my heart rate up.

I go jogging with my friend on the weekends. We signed up to do a 5K race together!

# LIFE WITH DIABETES

Diabetes can be hard for young people to manage. Most teens want to feel in control. Diabetes may make them feel like they're not in control of their own body.

Some insulin **regimens** need to be done at the same time every day. This means that sleeping in isn't always possible. Low blood sugar levels can also make it unsafe to drive. Having diabetes doesn't mean you can't have a job. But it does mean that you have to manage your diabetes.

People with diabetes sometimes worry they'll eat something wrong or be seen as different from their peers.

# Learn More!

**The CDC's National Diabetes Education Program**
https://www.cdc.gov/diabetes/ndep/people-with-diabetes/resources/for-children-teens.html

The Centers for Disease Control and Prevention provides children and teens with information on how to manage their diabetes.

- People with type 1 diabetes are more likely to develop an eating disorder.
- Drinking alcohol increases the risk of hypoglycemia. If someone with diabetes drinks alcohol, they may also forget to take their insulin.
- Smoking tobacco can increase blood glucose levels.
- Body piercings and tattoos can lead to infections. People with diabetes have a hard time fighting infections.

# DIABETES AT SCHOOL

Having to manage diabetes at school can feel overwhelming for newly diagnosed teens. Teachers want students to stay safe and healthy. The school will need a plan for how to help the student manage their diabetes during school hours.

The school nurse and teachers should know how to see and treat low blood sugar. Physical education teachers should also know what a student with diabetes needs to stay safe. It's also helpful for the student's close friends to know the warning signs of low blood sugar.

A medical ID tells emergency medical personnel, such as paramedics and law enforcement, that the person has diabetes. Without one, paramedics might not know what's wrong.

# Diabetes Medical Management Plan (DMMP)

**A DMMP has everything a school needs to know about how to manage a student's diabetes, including:**

- The student's insulin regimen, target blood glucose levels, and whether they need help checking their blood sugar
- The student's symptoms of hypoglycemia and how to treat it
- Insulin and other medications the student takes
- What the student can eat for meals and snacks
- How to manage exercise

## YOUR OWN "HYPO" BOX

A "hypo" box is a box of supplies needed in case someone has hypoglycemia. Students should keep one in the nurse's office. A "hypo" box may include:

- Glucagon (a medicine used to increase blood sugar levels quickly)
- Lancets (tiny needles used for blood sugar testing)
- Test strips
- Blood sugar monitor
- Glucose pills
- Juice boxes
- Crackers

# DIABETES AND FRIENDS

Managing diabetes is much easier with a support system. A support system includes parents, teachers, and friends. For young people, having supportive friends can be the difference between feeling overwhelmed and feeling confident.

The physical, mental, emotional, and social effects of diabetes are all connected. Teenagers with type 1 diabetes are more likely to manage their diabetes better when they have supportive friends. Sharing your diabetes story with a trusted friend can help you stay healthy for a long time.

People can show their support for their friends with diabetes by eating healthy foods and being active.

# Find a Community!

**American Diabetes Association**
https://www.diabetes.org/

The American Diabetes Association is a great resource for people looking for information and to find others who understand what they're going through. This website even directs you to local offices.

## WHAT CAN FRIENDS DO?

- Talk to your friend, a doctor, or a family member who has diabetes to learn the facts.
- Know that diabetes is different for everyone.
- Help your friend have healthy habits, such as eating healthy foods and drinking plenty of water.
- Give your friend time to manage their diabetes.
- Know the symptoms of hypoglycemia.

# GET HEALTHY, STAY HEALTHY

Making healthy choices isn't something only people with diabetes should do. Healthy choices can help everyone feel better physically and emotionally. Finding healthy foods and activities that you enjoy is a step in the right direction.

You can start making healthier choices right now. Instead of drinking a sports drink or a soda, drink water or coconut water. When you get home from school, take your dog for a walk instead of watching TV. Think about how these healthy choices will make you feel in the long run.

After a week or two of brisk walking, you might feel strong enough to go for a short run. Running is a great way to get your heart and lungs working. You might choose to join the cross-country or track team at school too!

Chapter 4

# Supporting Jenna

When I found out my best friend, Jenna, has type 1 diabetes, I was confused and a little shocked. I didn't know much about diabetes. Jenna told me how hard it was to keep it a secret for so long.

I remember noticing Jenna going to the nurse's office and bathroom a lot. It must be hard for her to keep up with friends and activities. Sometimes she has to check her blood sugar seven times a day!

Jenna worries a lot about what she eats. She also has to make sure she has all her supplies if she wants to go to a friend's house. I want to learn more about type 1 diabetes so I can support her.

Now that we're older, my friend is more open about her diabetes. She answers all our questions, even if they're kind of silly. We've all done our best to learn as much as we can about type 1 diabetes.

# DAILY ROUTINE

For someone with diabetes, checking their blood sugar is an important part of their daily **routine**. People usually check their blood sugar before and after they eat, before they go to bed, and while they exercise. Some people need to check their levels more often, especially if they're sick.

People can check their blood sugar levels anywhere using a blood glucose meter. It's a good idea to write down your levels in a notebook. Your doctor will want to see how your levels change over time.

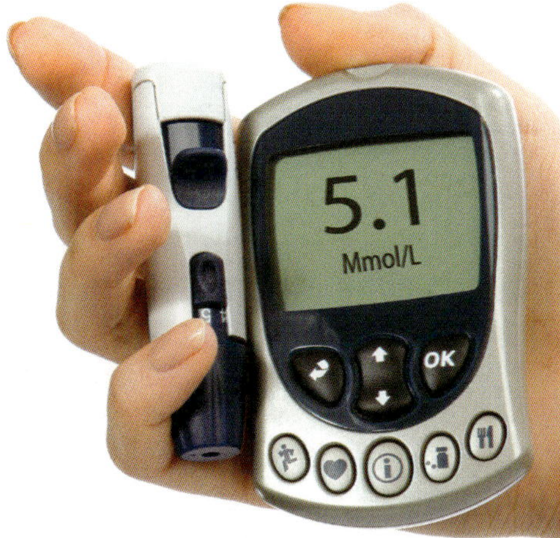

Some people manage their diabetes with insulin, pills or tablets, and glucagon along with a healthy diet and exercise. All people with type 1 diabetes and many people with type 2 diabetes need insulin every day. People with type 1 diabetes can't take pills or tablets. People with both types of diabetes can use glucagon.

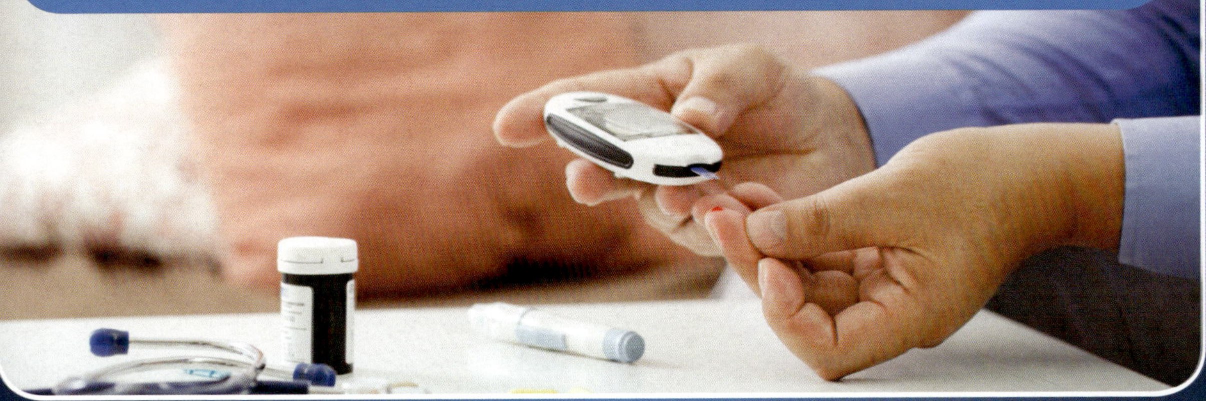

## HOW TO USE A BLOOD GLUCOSE METER

A blood glucose meter is a small computer that measures the amount of glucose in a sample of blood. Here's how it works:

- Put a new test strip into the glucose meter.
- Put a new lancet in your lancing device.
- Snap the needle into the tip of your finger and squeeze a drop of blood out.
- Apply the blood to the edge of the test strip.
- The meter tests the blood and shows your blood glucose level on the screen.

# PLENTY OF EXERCISE

Exercise helps everyone stay healthy. Diabetes doesn't keep people from exercising, and they can participate in the same sports and activities as everyone else. Staying active helps people's bodies use insulin. This means it's easier to manage their diabetes if they're active.

If you want to connect with other people who have diabetes, you can join the Beyond Type 1 Snail Mail Club. This is a pen pal program for kids and teens with type 1 diabetes around the world. On Beyond Type 1's website, you can also join a running or biking club.

https://beyondtype1.org/snail-mail-club/

Before someone starts to get active, they should speak with their doctor. They should be sure to drink plenty of water, check their blood sugar before and after they exercise, wear proper socks and shoes, and check their feet for any injuries.

## Beyond Type 1

When Nick Jonas was diagnosed with type 1 diabetes when he was 13 years old, he didn't have a community to support him. This made him feel alone. In 2007, he told the public about having type 1 diabetes. He cofounded Beyond Type 1, a **nonprofit** that teaches people about diabetes, fights for diabetes awareness, and supports finding a cure for diabetes.

**https://beyondtype1.org/**

# OTHER HEALTH PROBLEMS

Diabetes can cause other health problems. However, many of them are preventable as long as people manage their diabetes well, eat healthy foods, get plenty of exercise, and stay healthy otherwise.

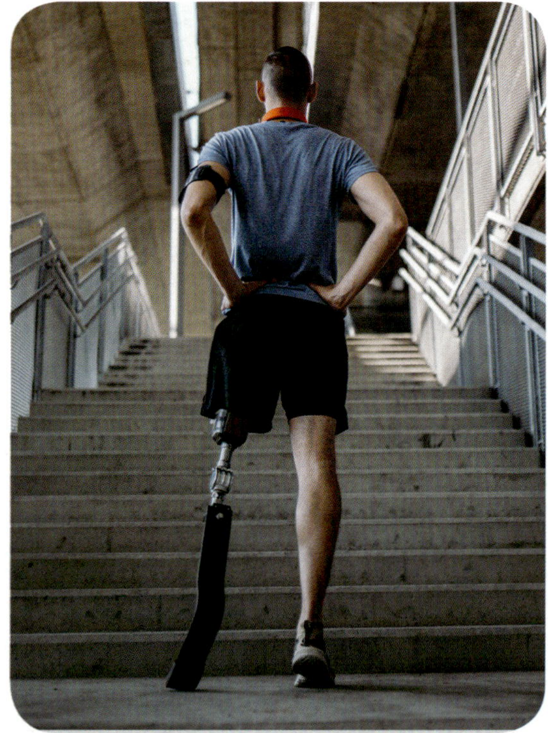

Neuropathy is damage to or disease of the nerves. It can damage people's limbs, which may result in them needing to have that limb amputated, or cut off.

If someone has high blood sugar over a long period of time, they may have problems with their eyes, kidneys, nerves, heart and blood vessels, or gums. Diabetes can also affect a person's mental health. Seeing a therapist or counselor can help improve mental health and manage diabetes.

## Diabetes Distress

Diabetes distress is a common mental health issue. People with diabetes distress may feel frustrated, sad, and tired of dealing with diabetes every day. If people feel sad or worried, they should ask their doctor to refer them to a therapist who specializes in chronic illnesses.

## HOW TO PREVENT COMPLICATIONS

- Follow your doctor's instructions on how to manage your diabetes.
- Don't smoke or drink alcohol.
- Schedule regular physicals and eye exams.
- Take care of your teeth.
- Check your feet daily for changes or injuries.
- Exercise regularly.

# LOOKING FORWARD

Before the discovery of insulin in 1921, many people with diabetes died soon after they were diagnosed. Today, people can live long, healthy lives if they manage their diabetes. This is all thanks to the hard work of doctors and researchers.

In 2018, 34.2 million people in the United States, or 10.5 percent of the population had diabetes. As of 2017, diabetes is the seventh leading cause of death in the United States. Doctors and researchers continue to develop better treatments for people with diabetes. They're also looking for a cure for diabetes.

Doctors and researchers are trying to figure out how to prevent diabetes in people who may have certain genes.

# GOING TO THE DOCTOR

People with diabetes who use insulin shots usually see their doctor at least every three to four months. The doctor wants to know how well the person is managing their diabetes. The doctor will also want to check for symptoms of complications.

Going to a general practitioner means that you'll be in charge of your health care. You should go to your first appointment prepared with questions for your new doctor.

People with diabetes can prepare for their doctor's appointment by bringing a record of their blood sugar levels. They should make sure to talk about any symptoms of hypoglycemia or hyperglycemia. Finally, they should tell their doctor about any new illnesses or symptoms.

## Changing Doctors

Most pediatricians, or doctors who treat children, stop seeing patients who are 18 to 21 years old. Changing from a pediatrician to a general practitioner, or doctor who treats people of all ages, can sometimes be difficult. Ask your pediatrician to suggest a general practitioner to help make the change easier.

## QUESTIONS TO ASK YOUR DOCTOR

- How often should I test my blood sugar? What if my blood sugar is too high or low?
- What kinds of symptoms should I look out for to prevent complications?
- What other doctors should I see regularly? An eye doctor? An endocrinologist?

Chapter 5

# Becoming Healthy and Confident

I've been so frustrated and worried since my diagnosis that I haven't been managing my diabetes very well. I decided to talk to my doctor about everything I've been thinking about and feeling.

My doctor recommended a great therapist who works with people who have diabetes. She's helped me find ways to manage my diabetes better. She also helped me connect with other teens who have diabetes.

I've learned a lot about diabetes. Explaining it to people and answering their questions doesn't make me feel different. It makes me feel empowered. I've realized how much I can do just by keeping my diabetes under control. Now that I've found a way to manage my diabetes, I'm finally looking forward to going to college.

I still have to test my blood sugar multiple times a day. But I've been doing it for so long now that I barely even have to think about it. My routine is important to me and I always have my supplies with me.

# GLOSSARY

**carbohydrate:** Any one of various substances found in certain foods, such as bread, rice, and potatoes, that provide your body with heat and energy and are made of carbon, hydrogen, and oxygen.

**cholesterol:** A type of fat made by the liver that is found in your blood. Cholesterol is also found in foods such as meat, dairy products, and fish.

**data:** Facts and figures, information.

**develop:** To bring out the possibilities of, to begin to have gradually, or to create over time.

**diagnose:** To identify a disease by its signs and symptoms.

**dietitian:** A person trained to give people advice about diet and nutrition.

**embarrassed:** Feeling or showing awareness for something you feel you've done wrong.

**emotionally:** In a way that has to do with emotions, or feelings.

**energy:** The power to work or to act.

**environment:** The conditions that surround a living thing and affect the way it lives.

**gene:** Tiny parts of a cell that are passed from parent to child and that decide features in the child, such as eye color.

**gland:** A body part that produces something that helps with a bodily function.

**hormone:** A natural substance produced in the body that controls the way the body develops.

**insulin:** A hormone in the body that helps process glucose, or sugar.

**nonprofit:** An organization that doesn't seek to make a profit, usually created for a public good.

**pancreas:** A body part near the stomach that produces insulin, the substance that helps the body use and break down food.

**physically:** In a way that has to do with the body instead of the mind.

**prevalent:** Common or widespread.

**regimen:** A plan or set of rules about something, such as food or exercise.

**routine:** A regular way of doing things in a particular order.

**stress:** Something that causes strong feelings of worry.

**symbol:** Something that stands for something else.

**virus:** A very small living thing that causes disease and spreads from one person or animal to another.

# INDEX